1970

Types of Shape
poems by John Hollander

Atheneum
New York 1969

Books by John Hollander

poetry   *Types of Shape 1969*
Visions From the Ramble 1965
Movie-Going 1962
A Crackling of Thorns 1958

criticism   *The Untuning of the Sky 1961*
Ideas of Music in English Poetry
1500-1700

for children   *The Quest of the Gole 1966*

John Hollander's first book of poems, *A Crackling of Thorns*, was chosen by W. H. Auden as the 1958 volume in the Yale Series of Younger Poets; *Moviegoing and Other Poems* appeared in 1962, and *Visions From the Ramble* in 1965. He wrote a book of criticism, *The Untuning of the Sky*, and edited both *The Laurel Ben Jonson* and, with Harold Bloom, *The Wind and the Rain*, an anthology of verse for young people, and an anthology of contemporary poetry, *Poems of Our Moment*. He is the editor (with Anthony Hecht) of *Jiggery-Pokery: A Compendium of Double Dactyls*. Mr. Hollander attended Columbia and Indiana Universities, was a junior fellow of the Society of Fellows of Harvard University, and taught at Connecticut College and Yale. He is now Professor of English at Hunter College, and last year was Overseas Fellow at Churchill College, Cambridge, England.

Acknowledgments: these poems originally appeared in
Partisan Review, Harper's Magazine, The Columbia University Forum, Alphabet, Lillabulero, Stereo Hi-Fi Review and *Poetry* (in which *Graven Image, Crise de Cœur, Broken Column, Swan and Shadow* and *Bell Curve* were first published).

Library of Congress catalog card number 68-9726
Published simultaneously in Canada by McClelland and Stewart Ltd
Printed at the Press of A. Colish, Mount Vernon, New York
Bound by H. Wolff, New York
Designed by Alvin Eisenman

First Edition

For James Merrill

Contents

I

Skeleton key

*Opening and starting key for a
1954 Dodge junked last year.*

O with what key
shall I unlock this
heart Tight in a coffer
of chest something awaits a
jab a click a sharp turn yes an
opening Out with it then Let it
pour into forms it molds itself
Much like an escape of dreaming
prisoners taking shape out in a
relenting air in bright volumes
unimaginable even amid anterior
blacknesses let mine run out in
the sunny roads Let them be
released by modulations
of point by bend of
line too tiny for
planning out back
in hopeful dark
times or places
How to hold on
to a part flat
or wide enough
to grasp was
not too hard
formerly and
patterned
edges cut
themselves
What midget
forms shall
fall in
line or
row beyond
this wall
of self A
key can
open a car
Why not me
O let me
get in

2

A possible fake

Black, undecorated bucchero cup,
cracked and mended,
Etruscan, bought in Rome 1963
with no questions asked.

I have given up caring whether youre genuine or not
now that I know what you have been through Slowly
shortening moments of course but the harsh snap
of the speeded-up instant and the rape of the
smooth black surface like a cracked shellac
record are authentic enough While you say
I TOO WAS EARTH ONCE STILL I YIELDED UP

FORMS POSSIBLE IN ME TO TURN MERE CUP
your fault your cracked base cannot
be seen from where I look and try
to read your heart And what you
say is true enough for mortals or
for earthen gods What bears
the weight of this so
pretentious
crown Is it
mere mire
column of
common or
even rare
clay that
carries a
proud cup
so dry so
empty now
Lo what the
potter twists
on his flat
turning wheel
is his idea and
a cup or an image
a poem or body that
turns beneath my hand O
beauty is no less true than you

3

Under the beach umbrella

At mid-day.

```
                            Straight
                    overhead now as white as
                  it ever gets and fiercer than we
              can imagine the sun threatens Not with a hot
            white eye but under a cupped palms dark plot to grow
          to extend the field of shadow still no wider than our spread
        of tented blue canvas Within this dark ring is no pain White beach
      burns unbearably beyond a hot line where the edge of the noons blade
                                  is
                                  as
                                  of
                                  an
                                  ax
                                  To
                                  go
                                  by
                                  it
                                  so
                                  as
                                  to
                                  be
                                  in
                                  or
                                  at
                                  or
                                  on
                                  it
                                  is
                                  to
                                  be
                                  of
                                  it
                                  as
                                  we
                                  all
                                  are
      even alas out of it within this fragile and shifting circle of shade
```

4

Idea

Old Mazda lamp, 50-100-150 W.

On or
off Either darkness
unlocked again or feigned
daylight perhaps graded only by
stepped intensities fifty watts apart
In any event no continuities like those
of flickering no nor even of fading Flick
Click and there it is suddenly Oh yes I see
Indeed A mind hung brilliantly upon filaments
stung by some untongued brightness opening up
also encloses and the dark unbounded room lit
by bare bulbs collapses into an unhurting box
occupied by furniture now avoidable The dot
of closure menaces the attention which in
the flutter of eyelids can only tremble
like a nervous child lying awake lest
he be aware of the moment a closing
shutter of sleep claps to But a
snapped—off dream disperses
into darkness like gold
becoming mere motes
becoming light If
the eye lies open
to such dust as
sunlight brings
it will never
burn But that
creation make
a visible big
difference in
the way minds
look a shaper
will burn
outwardly
first and
thus once
there was
light

5

Playing an obsolete instrument

Harpsichord, 1 manual,
by Hubbard and Dowd of Boston.
Drawn from memory.

For Ralph Kirkpatrick.

O
it
takes
too long
to tune and
looks far too
fragile to be
moved about a
world stocked
with disaster
too weak even
now to move a
freighted ear
Time untuning
everything of
tightness made
attentions slip
as it was played
for Olde Musickers
while Polyhymnia and
Clio fidgeted and seven
more wearied knowing girls
fussed with their hats But then
the silliness stopped When Orpheus
took up a tom—tom once visions and
order impinged on the landscape of
fragile but wiry dreams ringing in

          possibilities O now even
          tapping out syllables on
          a rounded rump is not as
          joyful or strong a music

6

Bell curve

Normal curve of distribution.

                    It is the
                   top which
                  seems to an
                eye untorn by tears a
               kind of base not from but
              on which the whole sounding
             body depends Up high the most
            frequent the most ordinary will
            bunch together there where mean
           and mode unite At such a height a
           tired watcher of bells might hope
            for far more sound for rounder or
           rarer tones O even there at the top
           for bright clear fundamentals where
          most normal noises are not of chiming
          but of clonk and thunk But no for the
          sound of ringing is only found in the
          massed metal below down there where all
          frequencies of bong bing and happenings
         are lower There where the bronzed embrace
        surrounds the heart of air the body sounder
        and the deep pounding partials far more tidal
       there at the widening there there the true bell
       sings all ringed about with bell-shaped roundness
     Whatever the pinched arch top may assert these wide
      so generous depths affirm nothing and thereby never lie
    Here at bell-level nearly at the lip of truth even a sigh
    will resound and trembling will be a proclamation The sound
    of an hour passing is that of another coming Unskewed by will
    or cracked by what in fact the case may be in the surrounding
                   air and
                  all it is
                  ringing O
                   hear it
                    now

7
Love letter

*Hand-set text capital, classical,
reminiscent of the
types of Didot and Bodoni,
with pronounced serifs.*

Love begins with
light Long
glances at
ladies who
even under
this stony
blue-white
ray or its
unwarm and
unalarming
shade form
the lovely
shapes are
the lances
that break
in through
the light-
filled and
resounding
valleys we
lie across
when touch
lengthened
by longing
leads us O
my love to
a darkness
we welcome
Left alone
we can lie
clasping a
gap on two
sides like
the letter
that means   —odd
half a square hundred dark places we lay in fifty ~~old~~
remembered times of light unending your beginning O Love

Help me
O help me for only
a brief while ago I hung red
and yet erect in the world of wide
white reticent backgrounds against which
I registered Correctly placed as if pointing
out a direction downwards towards which all must
fall I stood firm I beat out the cut time which we
always hope we have to count on More surely than as an
emblem cut into a thick-skinned tree transfixed by a dart
perhaps I shone and signified Being all crimson and heraldic
as I was and near-kin to the promiscuous scarlet pips of cards
I was unyielding and if conventional than surely constant But as
I stood in my round-shouldered pride you struck Some fell impulse
seized me as if for a moment the surface I clung to had gone blank
like that As if a glimpse of folded arm or breast or thigh curved
under itself plunging deep into its own shadow had unhung me quite
Or as if some loss as of dry leaves blown across marble corridors
was felt for an instant even while unseen I fell tripping over a
minute lapse in lifes surface I fell heavily ah indeed flipped
over and now I lie bleeding on my sheet a sick valentine who
short of breath can barely sigh BE MINE before I fail for
even the short while that will be forever Lying here I
have blackened some and paled Yet recognizable for
what I am and unable to leap I rest uneasy Fever
warms me up towards evening after failure of
nerve has made a noon too bright to bear
bringing in place of sleep a sense
of something wrong something
half-unbroken Like
a heart

9
Eskimo Pie

(Not to speak of Popsicle,
Creamsicle and the rest.)

I shall
never pretend
to have forgotten
such loves as those
that turned the dying
brightness at an end of
a childs afternoon into
preludes To an evening of
lamplight To a night dark
with blanketing To mornings
of more and more There deep
in the old ruralities of play
the frosted block with papery
whisps still stuck to it kissed
me burningly as it arose out of
dry icy stillnesses And there now
again I taste first its hard then
its soft Now I am into the creamy
treasure which to have tasted is to
have begun to lose to the heat of a
famished sun But O if I break faith
with you poor dreadful popsicle may
my mouth forget warm rains a tongue
musty Pauillac cool skin all tastes
I see
sweet
drops
slide
along
a hot
stick
It is
a sad
sorry
taste
which
never
comes
to an
end

Graven image

The shield of David,
of no great antiquity as a
liturgical symbol.

```
                                A
                               bit
                             of an
                            image a
                          hint only
                        a momentary
                      finial like a
                    barely-glimpsed
                  porpoise possibly
  thrusting a dark shining horn through the distant water These
    should plunge one into the deeps of significance where tall
      forms stand for their maker while tides throb vast beyond
        dreaming even overhead Craving the rich dark icons ever
        denied us one day I drew upon the flat wet sand above
          the menace of foamy conquerings this hexagram which
            with the broad menorahs feathered wings was all
              the symbol we were permitted But far from the
              water of summer the sea I would gaze at the
              woven equilaterals on the synagogue wall at
            the New Year their members joined arms locked
          in legs all fondly wrought and standing for and
        on the wall unshielding be it in blue or yellow O a
        flat emblem almost a blank But as a coupling of these
      identicals used so as to seem at war how much a sign of
    love Even here though the image dives down into the wider
  part to vanish into meaning Here too in my crude making the
end the remembered part before darkness marks a point of love
                      Let there be only
                        this final sign
                        this triangle
                          of the dark
                            about thy
                              opening
                                loves
                                  own
                                   V
```

II

Four-in-hand

In an exchange for a
wide, old silk one.

For Holly Stevens.

Not Gordian nor a
Ghiordes warped
onto a bright
bit of yarn
from a rug
hiding in
high pile
No this is

not somehow

the knot of

the quotidian

which with an

as yet unmashed

panache he ties

mirrored mornings

to himself with A

holding together of

all of the reins of

the real for a time

A constant feeling of

widely bright stripes

to bind him through a

general zebra barriness

that comes between word

and word with interlinear

blanks Are these his hearts

blinds Or the binds

that almost

tie

12

Domed edifice

Low Memorial Library,
named, but no longer serving as,
The Library of Columbia University.
By Charles F. McKim.
Completed 1897.

Columbia Phi Beta Kappa Poem, 1967.

Closure
surmounts the
strange open ways
that even an interior
may inherit or a dark chamber
achieve through partial ruin Such
unpierced coverings hold dominion for
ever over minded regions below as the
sky does above our heightened eyes that strive to measure
and contend Not like the sole fiery lord rising wide over
azure ramparts nor Madame M queen of all the minor purple
distances her dust penetrated her silver honor intact Not
like the stony rule of starlight raining in apertures cut
to admit the once-unruined gods But from this distance or
this angle our sunlit or unlit domes govern their domains
as a skull tells its soft protectorate I am clamped above
you for your own good and behold there is still visionary
room above you We have lain below we who scanning all the
unquiet ceilings of day and night know every zenith to be
limned on the inner surface of some one of our domes our many
unopening skies We have strained Our parched eyes water only by our
lowering of them into depths of darkness and touch toward our bottom doom

13

Vanished mansard

The top of Memorial Hall, Harvard,
completed 1874-6,
burned down September 6, 1957.

No views from here
but always visions
of it high and red
Even when it still
sprang majestic into
the winter air there
ornate and overlooking
all the green below with
an unattainable top that
leaped into so many raised
glances and crowned nearly
all our final backward gazes
And our first glimpse placed
a heroic symbol surely between
the leaves of remembrance Even
when we said The Albert Memorial
on top of the Albert Hall See it
was in knowing that as we stood in
its long shadow we were waiting at
the brink of its green moment of new
beauty phasing in on our age like an
ease of shading a tower tenders And as
Verena Tarrant confronted her Southern
challenger under its memorial woodenness
momentous Latin lifted her own momentary
air aloft So when like the travelling case
designed for a summit or climax or triumph
or surprise it burns even now backstage in a
decade-old theatre of reminiscences black flourishings
of smoke enfold again the splendid day as an abolished
clock strikes a muffled hour Ours it was And if towers
can be owned only by viewing with their eyes all they overshadow
then our dark hearts have had it all as our wide eyes have
overseen from white impatient towers claiming the skys
brightness without thrusting toward it the red of clay
New towers are for climbing This lost peak ascended us

I
can
point
where I
so desire
even aiming
backwards and
behind my head For who can say what I intend or mean to signify Does a
mere goal matter more than a source Does the promising arc of curved bow
not stand for more of what I mean than the childishly-colored face masking
the unresisting but unbending straw But what I may mean means nothing What I
say is what I am mistaken for Doomed by the human habits erasing eyes ever
to be a cheerful idiot I indicate the future only the failed vision of a
mere next thing a clear day a startling glance a New York State-shaped
poem on a new
page O mild
abandoned
regions
where
was
I

Some broken
Iroquois adze
pounded southward
and resembled this
outline once But now
boundaries foul-lines
and even sea-coasts are
naturally involved with
mappers and followers of
borders So that we who grew
up here might think That steak is
shaped too much like New York to be real And like
the shattered flinty implement whose ghost lives
inside our sense of what this rough chunk should
by right of history recall the language spoken by
its shapers now inhabits only streams and lakes and
hills The natural names are only a chattering and mean
only the land they label How shall we live in a forest of
such murmurs with
no ideas but in
forms a state
whose name
passes
for
a city

The figure in the carpet

*Geometrical version,
as in some Serabend and Herez rugs,
of the Boteh figure best known in
the West through Paisley prints.*

Those who use the
signs know them but
for what they are And
thus this flame or leaf
a fruit or yet unflowered
uterus this cupping fig and
tongue of fire at once thrust
up in measured ranks is knotted
into life and binding necessary
yarn gets snipped So So Thus if
we know this general boteh sign
as a palm of meanings stretched
out over half of Asia what then
of the primitive of one palm or
one leaf of light only who ties
what he thinks to what he makes
so gaily and unshakingly But as
our eyes must drop to interpret
the makers gaze meets his thing
with upraised face We squint at
floors and walls or admire what
lies behind glass in shops dark
glasses lifted in the shade And
when darkness erases bright
patterns shall even the
dim paradigm remain
for those who peer so after
significances When that
all goes the carpet
is obscured not
by darkness
but our
dust

17

Squares

For a vibrating, blue-on-red painting
by Reginald Pollack.

This one may hurt Not by
throbbing away at vision
only no nor in the glare
where wobbling knowledge
and bright uncertainties
prevail but back there O
deep behind the curtains
of sight in an innermost
final round dark theatre
the pain is caused by no
sharp—edged light but by
the pure noumenal square

No not luminosities here
warring across the wheel
where hues cry out as if
in outrage at each other
No it is the affront the
shimmering of dreams say
of possible planes gives
to steadier phenomena as
when a standing cone cut
by an unconsciousness of
shadow frightens one who
swims in towards a beach

18

Work problem

A note without even a clef.

For Leonard Bernstein.

Across the unruled steppes stretch endless whitenesses

                              If
then governing lines of driven idea and road reach out
                              as
                              in
                              an
opening up of arms too long folded toward destinations
                              in
                              us
                              we
can barely ever dream of how easy then to see how hard
                              it
                              is
                              to
violate those snowy distances those wide possibilities
                              by
                    crotchets or
                 in vaguenesses
              unkeyed Are we sounding
                 a c of noon Or
                    midnight E

19

Blots

Mistakes; losses.

For Alvin Eisenman.

                How did this ever happen
                Why gradually dear just
                as everything else does
                Like rivers cutting whitely
              and unexpectedly now through
               dark forests of prose or like
                widows left high atop
               shining pages of futurity the
            unpromising blob of language may
           reassume its visionary form
                leaving its track of utterance
                across a fecund surface finally to
                lie there a text in state awaiting
                death its scholia gathering like sculpted
                urns about it and all its great beasts
                of myth straining eternally at their
                leashes
                Or else
                it may
                 not

                And so we are left with our blotches our
                 formal horrors lying about in what cannot
                even be called pools drying into dark stains
               A painters random drip is licked up by
                some omnivore of dream and redeemed
                But our poor errors shooting out sudden pseudopods into nothingness that
                remain to reproach us like the panhandle
             of some long since abolished state
            are beyond changing We cannot even claim
            that a prior form of change came once when
             some nymph say with a lost or an unreadable
                  name fled the clutches of a ravishing
                   panic grasp and was led by a relenting god
                    into the dark safety of meaninglessness of
                    colors that read as shade only of shapes
                     that suggest no mind nor hand
                      behind their making
                       But alas these unsuccesses these
                       typos and botched
                       lineaments fill up
              the spaces of conjecture cutting with the needlessly
                         hard edges by which any
                       wretched but willful roadside sign says
                            EAT refusing to blend
                       like nonsense into the general the blue

20

Broken column

For William Arrowsmith.

```
                    Are
                    you
                    too
                    proud
                    to give
                    up what
                    you can
                    no longer
                    possess
                    Such an
                    embattled
                    final cause
                    as attempting
                    to support by
                    piling up stone
                    on baser stone a
                    high impediment
                    to windiness is
                    bound to be blown
                    down Down there an
                    airy will must get
                    serious as winds
                    that can no more
                    than whisper about an
                    unyielding wish still
                    do their bit as brick
                    falls to extractions as
                    carious rocky drums go
                    smash and unfilled chunks
                    of jagged marble mark out on
                    one side the direction that a
                    disaster may take Thrusting up
                    from springing green wide lawn
                    and clusterings of acanthus an
                    assertive spike of white comes
                    bearing no capital no unbroken
                    shaft The ruin of your highest
                    and most visionary part may be
                    a burden at your age not worth
                    maintaining Yet under the late
                sunlight your cold shadow falls across
               the meadow that has reassumed your shining
                  terraces across our own daughters tiny
        and blonde playing in and out of light Why gaze at
        blue perhaps then green beyond What further shores
        and what ever-unbroken marble do you strain to see
```

A view of the Untersberg

Elev. 6,000 ft.,
sw of Salzburg, as seen
through a window
in Schloß Leopoldskron.

```
                                    I
                                  stand
                              high on what
                             was once Odins
                           mound of power Held
                         breath comes slowly leaks
                      out toward high distant snows 0     I
             gasp     Grasped railings sang out in the harping
         of summit air before we both reached this point After all
        our downwardings so will they ever But now our view is toward the
       white abandoned heights of distant and unreached glaciers and even to fancy
     touching them is to be lost Behind us the planar prospects reveal their plantings
  of unmown hay their beliefs that rise up to this hill only in doing strange things still
 with fires on fall nights that one day Karl der Grosse may rise again from his sleep here
 to conquer the mountain ghosts They haunt us too not from the summit or the climb no from
 the bottom and the distance away that encases this height in rectangular frames of window
 There they are at night the red ambiguous beacon at the Geireck peak and the wan necklace
 of lights that marks the cable-car at unhappy Berchtesgaden But here on the plain again 0
 here at the bottom of the day we are changed by having been on that unreal height summits
 being what they are beyond Shifting attainable lying horizons are but as useful as dreams
```

High upward

*Through an uncelestial old
brass folding telescope.*

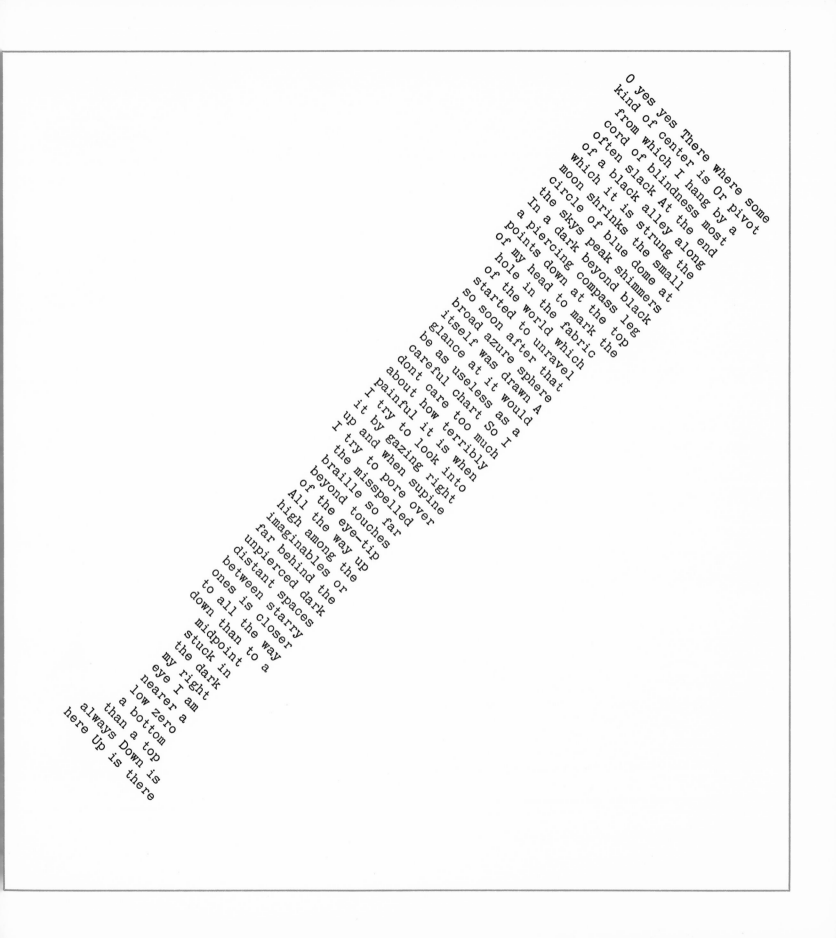

O yes yes There where some
kind of center is Or pivot
from which I hang by a
cord of blindness most
often slack At the end
of a black alley along
which it is strung the
moon shrinks the small
circle of blue beyond black
the skys peak shimmers
In a dark beyond black
a piercing compass leg
points down at the top
of my head to mark the
hole in the fabric
of the world which
started to unravel
so soon after that
broad azure sphere
itself was drawn A
glance at it would
be as useless as a
careful chart So I
dont care too much
about how terribly
painful it is when
I try to look into
up and when supine
it by gazing right
I try to pore over
the misspelled
braille so far
beyond touches
of the eye-tip
All the way up
high among the
imaginables or
far behind the
unpierced dark
distant spaces
between starry
ones is closer
to all the way
down than to a
midpoint
stuck in
the dark
my right
eye I am
nearer a
low zero
a bottom
than a top
always Down is
here Up is there

23

Last quarter

No new moon in its arms,
and yet, and yet . . .

```
                                        When
                                   parentheses
                                appear to be
                              opening then
                            beware of an
                          ending Never
                        misread such
                      signs as the
                    bold crescive
                   Cs of becoming
                  or of initials
                 curving toward
                the words like
               Come Clear Cup
              Changes Comedy
             Crystal Create
            or even Crowns
           Their openings
          stand only for
         closings As if
        our cupped left
       hands held out
      sickle-like to
     cradle a round
    towers bulbous
   copper top cut
  some blue some
 room some hope
out of the skys
 fierce surplus
 so these C-like
  marks close up
  But C-creatures
   grow yea truly
    behind and yet
     beyond limits
      So unrealities
       conclude in an
        eclipse of old
         moonlights by
          the darknesses
           of origin Here
            where the horn
             of light thins
              out into what
               is almost gone
                or lost a new
                 form starts as
                  a part of life
                      begins
```

24

Tekiah Gedolah

*The Last Horn-Blast, the longest
and final of the sequence of calls
blown on the* shofar *or ram's horn,
at the New Year.*

In memory of Noah Greenberg.

Who will understand its
rising intonation How
shall anyone not hear
Why will some try to
bear to listen Shall
a trumpet be blown in
a city and the people
be not afraid Or will
the first instant last
so long that many high
windy cornices housing
the self-emptying echo
of answers unrequested
will crumble before the
smiling silences regain
their rule Will her hair
throb Will his heart itch
Or will their eyes cloud
up when their ears stop
singing In a twilight
dying winds of blast
disperse in choirs
But with no west
where Over
To choke off

25

Swan and shadow

The last shape.

                    Dusk
                Above the
          water hang the
                    loud
                    flies
                    Here
                    O so
                    gray
                    then
                    What   A pale signal will appear
                    When   Soon before its shadow fades
                    Where   Here in this pool of opened eye
                    In us   No Upon us As at the very edges
                of where we take shape in the dark air
                  this object bares its image awakening
                    ripples of recognition that will
                        brush darkness up into light
even after this bird this hour both drift by atop the perfect sad instant now
                        already passing out of sight
                    toward yet—untroubled reflection
                  this image bears its object darkening
                  into memorial shades Scattered bits of
                  light   No of water Or something across
                  water   Breaking up No Being regathered
                  soon   Yet by then a swan will have
                    gone   Yes out of mind into what
                    vast
                    pale
                    hush
                    of a
                    place
                    past
          sudden dark as
                if a swan
                    sang